Kevin Leslie was brought up in Sydney, Australia, and moved to Adelaide in 1985. He has always loved being outdoors and going on camping trips with family and friends. He has worked in the camping industry for over 30 years, and this, his first book, is a result of many years of travelling in the Australian bush.

## Dedication

To my father, Roger, who passed away in 2009. We had some
great times together.

Kevin Leslie

# CARAVANNING AND CAMPING IN AUSTRALIA

AUSTIN MACAULEY PUBLISHERS™

LONDON • CAMBRIDGE • NEW YORK • SHARJAH

A CIP catalogue record for this title is available from the British Library.

ISBN 9781788485258 (Paperback)
ISBN 9781788485265 (Hardback)
ISBN 9781788485272 (E-Book)

www.austinmacauley.com

First Published (2018)
Austin Macauley Publishers Ltd™
25 Canada Square
Canary Wharf
London
E14 5LQ

# Introduction

Dad drove for a brewing company in Sydney as a contract driver, delivering beer and spirits to the many pubs and clubs across the city. He loved camping and liked to take my mother, my sister and me along with him. He owned his own truck and would put a set of high frames, called gates, around the tray of the truck and cover them with a heavy canvas tarp. This was where we all slept on canvas stretchers.

We had a small black car which was also transported on the back of the truck. When we got to our destination, Dad would unload the car by backing it down some ramps. This would enable us to drive around the area or to the shops, without having to move the truck. This was my introduction to camping. I was very little then, and have grown up loving camping ever since.

Over the years, I have camped in caravans and tents of various shapes and sizes, several motor homes, a bus that I fitted out, under tarps stretched over cars, in cars, in the back of different trucks, and in the open. When I was still at home, my father and I often went camping. My mother and sister decided it wasn't for them, so it was usually Dad and me, and often some friends would join us. We had some great trips together and I have such fond memories of our camping adventures.

The best of all was when, in 1986, I was on a working holiday around Australia, and dad and some friends joined me for a trip up Cape York Peninsula in Queensland. We travelled together for around five weeks. It was the last camping trip Dad and I had together.

Camping isn't for everyone. You will be exposed to the environment, and this will include sun, wind and rain. You may get your hands dirty and even get wet or muddy. You will also, at times, have to share toilet and shower facilities, and some of these may leave a lot to be desired.

With some planning and preparation, you can avoid all the problems and bad weather, in fact, in all the years that I have travelled and camped my way around Australia, there have only been a handful of times that things didn't go so well. It is a great way to see Australia and experience the great outdoors. You can get as close to nature as you like, see some wonderful flora and fauna, and visit some spectacular places. If you think it may be for you, then I suggest you try it at least once. You just might enjoy it.

# Chapter One
## Planning

Australia covers some 7.5 million square kilometres. The country is diverse, to say the least, with tropical coastal forests, rolling farmland, mountain ranges, vast plains, and outback deserts. The amount of planning and preparation required will, of course, depend on the length and type of trip you want to do. Simple weekends away are easy to plan, but planning for extended travel is much more involved.

Because Australia is so big, distances can seem a little daunting to travellers that have come from countries that are much smaller. Also, locals that have never travelled further than the airport will find the country a whole lot bigger than they thought.

When planning a trip, you should first look at how far you will be travelling, and how far apart services such as, petrol stations, food stores and accommodation are. This is not too big of a problem in coastal areas, as they are more populated. Particularly on the east coast. Towns are reasonably close together, and there is also good mobile phone reception, so keeping in contact is easy to do.

Of course there can still be big distances to cover, so allowances have to be made for travelling time and costs. Fuel is the single biggest cost, and it is surprising how much fuel will be required. In remote areas fuel can be almost double the price than in the cities.

Populated areas generally have good roads which enable travelling at highway speeds, therefore cutting down on time spent getting to your destination. There is also a greater selection of accommodation or camp grounds to choose from, as well as things to see and do.

Travelling through the interior, though, requires much more detailed preparation. Distances between services will be far greater than in populated areas, even on main highways it is not uncommon to travel around two hundred kilometres at a time, only to arrive at a solitary roadhouse, then travel a similar distance to the next one. And in between there is a whole lot of nothing, except dry arid country. This is the Australian outback.

I work in a camping store, and I often talk to people who have never been camping in any way, shape, or form. There is such a huge range of camping equipment to choose from; tents, bedding, camp-stoves, etc. Also, different options of caravans, camper trailers, motorhomes and more. It would be very easy to become confused and possibly make the wrong choice.

Before you go spending your money, ask yourself a couple of simple questions. Like, how many people are going, how long you are planning to go away for, will you be touring or just staying in one place? The answers to these questions will help you decide what gear you need and what you may not need.

Don't be tempted to over spend, but also don't buy anything too cheap. Equipment failure at a crucial moment is not fun. Try not to buy more than what you need, taking too much gear because you "might" need it is an easy trap to fall into. You end up with lots of stuff you never use. The best way is to follow the KISS method, which means "Keep It Simple Stupid".

For your first couple of trips, keep them short, and go to an established campground not too far from home with facilities, especially if you have children. This will give you a taste of what it's like in a comfortable environment that won't cost a lot of money. Then, if you like it, you can get more adventurous and try a bit further afield. Even to the extent of bush camping.

Camping with a tent is possibly the most economical way to introduce yourself to camping. A lot of camping gear can be hired, so you won't end up with having to sell things that you don't like.

Also, ask around and see what other people do. Different people have different ideas, consider what you learn, but in the end, use your common sense. Online reviews are a good way to see what other people have experienced and what gear they have used and what worked or what didn't.

You may think the tent is all you need, which is the case for a lot of people. However, if you want to get something better, then there is a whole lot of options open to you.

# Chapter Two
## What to Choose

## Motor Homes

The largest options are Motor Homes. Brand new, they tend to be more expensive than most caravans and campers, as you are not only buying a big comfy camper, but the vehicle that is under it as well. They are usually built on a small truck and are mounted permanently behind the cab, directly onto the chassis. The size of the truck may vary from small to medium to sometimes quite large, and the camper body will vary as well. Some of these vehicles will incorporate the cab into the motor home body, like those seen in America. Busses can also be fitted out as motor homes as well.

Depending on your needs and tastes, motor homes can be very simple or very luxurious and spacious. The larger ones are good for long-term trips, especially for families. They sit well on the road and can be easier to reverse than a caravan. However, the bigger ones can be a little difficult to manoeuvre into parking spots, because of their size, and if they are above a certain weight, you may need a heavy vehicle license to drive them. Smaller motor homes are much more popular, as they can still be very comfortable without the cost and size issues of the larger ones.

## Campervans

An alternative to a motor home is a campervan. This is where a small panel van is fitted out as a camper, a VW Kombi is a classic example. They have all the usual fittings, stove, fridge, bed, dinette, etc. same as the motor homes, but a lot more compact.

They are cheaper to buy, and easier to drive, and come in petrol and diesel, with manual or automatic transmissions. Some people use them as a second car. They offer better economy than their bigger brothers, but because of their small size, they are better suited to either one or two people.

Motor homes and campervans do have one disadvantage however, and that is if you decide to go out for a bit of sightseeing, you will need to pack it all up and take it with you, then set up again when you get back. Some people overcome this by taking pushbikes or motorbikes mounted on the back. Some with bigger vehicles, tow a small car on a trailer or an A-frame, or even occasionally hire a small car for the day. This is something you would have to consider before you purchase a motor home or campervan.

# Towing

By far the most popular way to tour Australia is with a caravan. From very small to absolutely huge, there is a caravan to suit almost everyone. Some manufacturers will even custom build a van to suit your needs and tastes. The choice is only limited to your imagination and wallet size.

It would be very easy to become lost in the myriad of choices when looking for a caravan, so better to start at the basics. Probably the first thing you should look at is your car.

Australian law says that you cannot tow anything above the vehicle manufacturers rated towing capacity. Simply put, if your vehicle has a rated towing capacity of say 2000kg, then that is the maximum amount that any trailer can weigh while being towed by that vehicle on any public road. Modifying your vehicle with bigger tyres, stronger springs, or engine modifications will not change the rating.

There is also a download rating, which is the amount of weight that can be carried by a towbar at the rear of a car. The towbar that is fitted to the car should also have the same ratings as the car. This can vary, but as a guide it would be approximately ten to fifteen per cent of the loaded weight of the van. However, this is not always the case, so you should check all the ratings of your car before buying any caravan. I have seen people turn up to pick up their brand new caravan, in a brand new car that cannot tow the van.

There should always be more weight on the front of the van than the rear, as it helps keep the trailer stable when travelling along the road. If there was more weight on the back of the van than the front, then it would be less stable and more likely to sway. This can lead to uncontrollable swaying, and ultimately loss of control, which can result in a nasty accident.

When a caravan is put on a towbar of a car, usually the back of the car goes down and the front goes up. The amount of movement between the back and front of the car, will vary depending on the weight of the caravan and the size and type of car. This would be more evident in a sedan or station wagon, but less so in a four-wheel drive.

In some cases, it may be necessary to fit weight distributing bars between the car and caravan. These are often called stabilising bars, load levellers, or anti-sway bars. The bars are fitted into a bracket that is fitted to the tow bar of the car, then lifted up under tension and put into pivoting cradles on the drawbar of the caravan. This has the effect of moving some of the weight of the front of the caravan to a point further forward on the car, therefore lifting the rear of the car and lowering the front. The result gives a more stable towing setup with better handling and a far lesser risk of uncontrollable swaying. You will always feel some movement between the tow vehicle and trailer, but better to keep it within controllable levels.

# Caravans

The size of the caravan depends on the individual requirements of the buyer. You may have children or just yourself and your partner. Some people buy bigger vans because they like the extra space. If you want a larger van, then you may have to upgrade your car with something that has a higher towing capacity, which can add considerable cost to the exercise.

In Australia we basically have two types of vans. There is the conventional caravan, and there is the pop-top caravan.

A pop-top caravan is where the roof sits on spring loaded cross arms or gas struts. When inside the van, the roof can be pushed upwards to a height similar to that of a conventional caravan. Around the perimeter of the roof there is a vinyl or canvas sleeve that fills the gap between the roof and sides of the van. There are usually large zippered panels in this sleeve which improve ventilation as well.

Pop tops are good for storing under low carports and garage doors. They may offer less wind resistance as well, because of their lower roof line. However, they won't necessarily be any lighter than a conventional caravan of similar size, they also won't be much longer than five or six meters. There are a few reasons for this but mostly because the roof, being much bigger, would become too heavy to lift up.

Conventional caravans on the other hand have a fixed roof and can be much longer. They usually have more storage space in the form of overhead cupboards, and it is easier to fit showers and toilets in.

Also, air conditioner units can be roof mounted which circulate the air better than the split system units found in pop tops, which also take up valuable cupboard space. Conventional caravans are better insulated than pop tops, because the walls, being full height, seal the van completely. In a pop top, the sleeve between the roof and sides offers very little insulation.

Caravans do have a downside though, and that is you have to tow it. You also have to store it somewhere when not in use, and you will have to park it. And (dread the thought) at some point you will have to reverse it into a campsite.

In reality, all this can be overcome with a little planning and practise. You can even get some instructions from various driver training companies, especially in the reversing department.

If you are looking at a caravan, then I urge you not to go out and buy the biggest one possible without some experience in towing. Remember, some vans can weigh more than your car, so you will have to make allowances for the bulk of the caravan behind you. Cornering needs to be taken a little wider than normal, and a bit more space is required for stopping and overtaking. Your car will work harder and will use more fuel.

Caravans come in on-road and off-road models and some are better suited to rough roads than others. However, they do have their limits. They're weight can be a problem especially in soft sand, with the van acting like an anchor, and body overhung behind the wheels can mean getting "hung up" with the rear digging into the ground, when you go through deep gutters or creek crossings. This means you get stuck and not able to go forward or backward.

## Fifth Wheeler

Another type of what could be called a caravan is a fifth wheeler. While the body is the same as a caravan, the difference is that instead of being towed behind the car with a drawbar, the front is supported directly on the back of either a utility, or tray top vehicle on a turntable. The wheels also sit much closer to the rear of the trailer, giving an overall appearance of a small semi-trailer.

A fifth wheeler is actually easier to reverse and will be far more stable on the road than a caravan, however, because their wheels are further back, they won't pivot as well as a caravan when turning and will require a little more space to manoeuvre. Depending on how big the unit is, it may also be necessary to use a small truck to tow it because of the weight at the front.

Caravanning is a very popular way to see our country, but if a caravan is not for you then you could look at a camper trailer.

## Camper Trailers

The camper trailer is a very close second in popularity, as it is cheaper to buy and easier to tow. Because they are also generally lighter, almost any car can tow one without needing towing aids.

Camper trailers (sometime called tent trailers) can be soft floor or hard floor. The soft floor has a tent section fitted on top of a normal trailer. This folds out to the side of the trailer down to the ground and forms a full height tent with a double bed on top of the trailer, with storage underneath the bed. Hard floor campers are a more dedicated trailer with a hard lid that folds out to the rear with the lid becoming the floor.

These trailers can vary greatly in design. Some are basic and you will need to take along camping gear as well, where others have slide-out kitchens, with everything you need; on board batteries, solar panels, water tanks, external lockers, etc. Once again they can be on-road and off-road.

The off-road models are very popular with four-wheel drive owners, as they are much easier to tow off road than a caravan, and once the basic unit is set up, an annexe can be added for extra room.

Some camper trailers have a wind up roof. Depending on the model, this type of camper can sleep up to six people. They are a bit of a cross between a caravan and a camper trailer with the inside similar to a caravan. They have a small kitchen with a stove, a fridge, a dinette and a few cupboards for storage. These units consist of a solid roof that is lifted up into place using a winch, located in the front of the body, and internal cables along with pushrods all cleverly hidden from view. Canvas walls with plastic windows are between the roof and the top of the side walls with pull out beds at each end, which are also under the canvas. And you can also fit an annexe to the side

A camper trailer will take longer to set up than a caravan. How much longer, will depend on the camper you have bought, and if you need the annexe. But most people cope with this and will get a routine together, which will quicken the set up process.

# Slide on Campers

Squeezed in somewhere between caravans and camper trailers are the slide on campers. In this case you would need a utility type vehicle with either a tub or flatbed at the rear, which the camper sits on. Although some are, the camper body isn't always fitted permanently to the vehicle, and can be raised off the vehicle with jacks and supported on stands, allowing the vehicle to be driven out from underneath. When required, the vehicle can be moved under the camper where it is lowered back on ready for use.

Some of these units have all the usual fixtures and fittings of a caravan, and will extend over the cabin of the car where the double bed is usually placed. However, the most popular types are fitted to four-wheel drives, and look more like a box. These units have various side lockers and drawers that are used for storage, as well as slide out kitchens and fridges with work benches and sinks. An awning can be fitted to the side for protection from sun and rain, and in some cases a tent as well, if needed.

Depending on the size and design, a slide on can be heavy, if it is more than the rated load capacity of your vehicle, then it will be illegal to drive it on the road because the vehicle will be overloaded. So check the weight before you purchase one.

If your budget doesn't stretch to a motor home, caravan or camper trailer, then there is always a tent.

## Tents

The most common type of tent you see today is the dome tent. From small to family size, they have been around for a long time and you will still see them in use in every campground. Erection time varies from about fifteen minutes to almost an hour.

The bigger the dome the longer it will take, because of the number of poles involved and having to assemble the poles first. You then have to thread them through the sleeves in the tent. After standing the tent up you still have to attach the fly section over the whole lot and peg it down. A dome tent will not be as stable as some other types due to the flexibility of the fiberglass poles and will move around a lot more in strong winds. The real advantage though, is the low cost in purchasing one compared to other tent designs.

Another type of tent that is getting more popular is an instant up tent, more commonly called touring tents. There are numerous manufacturers making these tents, with different sizes available to suit almost every situation.

Here, the tent is already fixed to the frame. The frame opens up outwards and upwards taking only minutes. A fly still has to be put on over the tent and tied down, but in most cases a touring tent can be erected in around fifteen minutes and dismantled in about the same, while there are different methods of opening the frame, the principle is the same.

Touring tents usually have steel or aluminium frames, so tend to be reasonably strong, and will stand up to bad weather better than other tents. You will pay more for this type of tent though, due to the construction and better fabrics used.

Most tents are made of polyester, but there are still lots of canvas tents around. While canvas may be stronger and more durable, they will be heavier and more expensive. Also canvas needs drying out before storing away, as mould can grow and cause the canvas to deteriorate.

Polyester on the other hand will be lighter and cheaper, and not so susceptible to damage by mould. Though they still need to be dried out before storage.

If a tent is your choice, take the time to look around at the different types and sizes. Consider how many people will sleep in it, and buy a tent that is rated one person more than what is needed. For example, if there are three sleeping in the tent then get a tent suited to four people. This will give you a little more space for personal items. Also, think about two smaller tents rather than one big one.

Budget wise, the dome tent still gives good value for money considering the amount of floor space you get compared to what you pay.

# Swags

If you really want to keep things simple, then a swag may be for you. Originally just a sheet of canvas that was laid out on the ground with a few blankets for a bed. If the weather became a bit damp, the side of the canvas was pulled over the top of the occupant to give some weather proofing.

Swags today, however, are more like a small tent. With poles to keep its shape, a zippered canvas top with flyscreen, are available in single, king single, double and extra wide models. Some swags are very simple resembling a canvas envelope, others are more elaborate with side entrances, ridge poles and various pockets for storing small items.

The swag comes with a mattress; however, it can be a little soft. People often have an extra mattress that they add for more comfort. Some people also keep their bedding in their swag so when they roll it up, it is all contained in one parcel. Then when unrolled, it is ready to hop into with little fuss.

Because there is some assembly required, they aren't that much faster to set up than a small tent, and in wet weather you would also need extra cover in the form of an awning of some sort to put the swag under, as they offer no protection from the elements unless you are in it, in bed.

Swags are still very popular and some people swear by them for their simplicity. But because they are canvas, you will find they can be an expensive piece of gear, also when rolled up, they can be very bulky taking up a lot of space in your car.

With all the different ways to go camping there are always variables to consider. So do some research and seek advice, and you should end up with the right gear to suit your type of camping.

# Chapter Three
## Safety

Road conditions will vary much more in the outback, with some "highways" being dirt roads, rather than sealed roads. Other secondary roads can be a bit rough, and other minor roads can be a nightmare with dust, corrugations, creek crossings and rocky outcrops. All this will add considerable time to your journey and also increase fuel consumption. In some cases, it may be necessary to carry extra fuel in jerry cans. There are a range of sizes and shapes available for carrying fuel, the important thing is you use an approved container, making sure it doesn't leak, especially if it is carried inside your vehicle. It would be advisable to do some research about this, as each state may have their own set of laws that covers carrying extra fuel in containers.

Try to plan your trip so you have several stops through the day. This will prevent driver fatigue, which can lead to falling asleep at the wheel with disastrous consequences. Taking turns driving with the other occupants of the vehicle is a good idea, this way everyone gets to drive and rest, especially on those long stretches of straight roads that you will find in the outback.

Night driving can be hazardous though, with wildlife or livestock wandering onto the road and being dazzled by headlights. Hitting any animal will not only be distressing (you may have to put the animal out of its misery), but a large animal can seriously damage your vehicle and cause a nasty accident.

Dirt roads at night can be very hazardous due to dust being thrown up by other vehicles. Passing a Road Train in these circumstances can mean being completely blinded by dust for almost a full minute. This can also happen during the day.

If a large vehicle is approaching you on dirt roads, reduce your speed, and put your headlights on, wait until you can see clearly before continuing. Slowing down can also prevent stone damage from the rocks that are thrown up by the truck's wheels.

If a road train comes up behind you and needs to pass, once it has pulled out to overtake, reduce your speed slightly and keep your vehicle steady. It will make it easier for the truck driver and you. Always use common sense, don't suddenly brake in front of these trucks, as they are very heavy and can't stop anywhere near as fast as a small vehicle can. Large trucks are not monsters, they are driven by real people that have families, and want to get home safely just like the rest of us.

Wherever you plan to travel in Australia, there are basic preparations that need to be carried out before you leave. Your vehicle needs to be mechanically sound and up to the task. A clapped out bomb is asking for trouble. Recovery costs can be high, in the thousands of dollars. Repairs can also be expensive as well as time consuming, as parts may have to be flown or trucked in, depending on where you are.

Take a few spare parts such as fan belt, spare hoses, fuel filter, extra fuses etc. Remember the more remote the area you are in, the more parts you should take. Carry some basic tools to carry out any repairs, and try to get some practical experience if you can, by doing a car maintenance course. Or at least get someone that knows how to show you.

Get your vehicle checked out by a competent qualified mechanic, there are numerous workshops that specialise in this. The same goes for any trailer or caravan you may be towing.

The vehicle and trailer needs to suit the type of roads that will be travelled. Taking a family sedan and caravan into the outback is fine, as long as it stays on sealed roads or good dirt roads. However, if you plan to travel to out of the way places, the roads may get a little rough. This is where you need a four-wheel drive. These vehicles have higher ground clearance, and a greater load capacity. Also, having a four-wheel drive will come in handy if road surfaces get a little slippery or soft.

A good set of tyres to suit the type of roads you will travel on is mandatory, and if you are travelling on a lot of dirt roads, a second spare wheel should be taken, as well as an extra one for any trailer if you are towing one, also take a good jack that has a rating of at least two tonnes.

Scissor type jacks are not suitable. They may be fine for your average car in town, but for a loaded 4WD, they are not strong enough, hydraulic or screw jacks are a better idea. A base plate to sit the jack on should also be carried. This gives the jack a flat solid surface to sit on. It helps keep the jack up straight, preventing it from falling over or from sinking into the ground if you're on a soft surface. Usually a piece of thick plywood about 35 cm by 35 cm or something similar will do the job.

One of the reasons why some people perished in the early days, was that if you became stranded somewhere, it was impossible to let anyone know you needed help. Communications were very limited then, but these days, things like portable two-way radios, satellite phones, and personal locator beacons are easy to access and use. Thanks to modern technology, there would be very few reasons why the outback traveller would not be able to call for help if they needed to.

Travelling with another vehicle is another way to ensure safety as well as letting a responsible person know where you are travelling and when you would be arriving at your destination. That way if you are overdue, it would be easier for authorities to look for you if they know where to look.

Don't forget to let your contact know you have arrived though, otherwise they may start a huge search effort for no reason. This may attract costs and fines to you!

Carry enough fuel, food, and importantly, water, to get you to where you are going, as well as a reasonable amount in reserve. Even in winter, temperatures can get higher than what you may think. If you do get into difficulty, then do not leave your vehicle. A car is easier to see from the air than a single person wandering around in the bush. Even disabled, your vehicle can offer you protection from the elements, and you can burn parts of it, e.g. seat covers, carpets, etc. to attract attention.

Having a campfire is a great way to not only cook dinner but to sit around and relax. But Australia is a very dry place. Bush fires can be devastating to land owners, towns and people's lives. I have seen some campfires resembling a towering inferno that uses huge amounts of wood. This often results in stripping areas bare of ground timber, which small animals use as their homes, and can create a dangerous situation if suddenly winds come up, blowing sparks into tinder dry bush. Keep campfires to a reasonable size that is easy to control and extinguish if necessary. Have an extinguisher or bucket of water close at hand, as well as a shovel, just in case. And observe any fire restrictions.

Regardless of where in Australia you will be travelling through, taking these simple precautions may save you a lot of money, time, and in some cases may save you from having to abandon your trip altogether. They may even save your life.

# Chapter Four
## What to Take

One problem that a lot of people who camp suffer from, is taking too much gear. It is important to look at what you will actually use in your day-to-day activities while camping. Of course this will change depending on what sort of camping you are doing, as well as how many people are going with you, age and even special needs have to be considered.

Let's say you have your vehicle of choice, and all is well and prepared as I have already mentioned. So let's now look at the basics. Caravans and campers already have beds, stoves, lighting, fridges, etc. But if you are in a tent or swag, then these are all extra.

# Bedding

Bedding is important to get right, because we all need a good night's sleep. Self-inflating mats and air mattresses are the usual way to go, remembering an air mattress also requires a pump of some sort, whereas self-inflating means just that. They have valves on one end which, when opened, allow the mattress to expand and fill with air. This is because the mattress is filled with a foam rubber type of material which reacts like a sponge and springs back into shape after it is compressed. When the mattress has fully inflated, the valves are closed and it is ready to use.

An old favourite is the camp stretcher, which is still proving to be very popular amongst campers. It is most popular with the older generation, as some people find it hard to get up and down to ground level, and a stretcher offers a good height to easily get in and out of bed. A stretcher takes up a bit more room in a tent than a mattress on the ground, and unfortunately, like air mattresses, they will not insulate you from the cold air underneath, as a self-inflating mat would. So it would be necessary to have a good blanket underneath you to help keep you warm on those extra chilly nights.

For bedding, some people prefer sheets and blankets like at home. In a motor home or caravan this is easier, as it is not necessary to make the bed each day. But for other types of camping, the bed has to be made and unmade every time you move.

Sleeping bags are ideal for this, as they only have to be unrolled and they are ready to use. Get a bag that suits the climate you are going to. Aim for one that is going to be warm. If it gets too warm, then the bag can be tossed off you and a lighter blanket can be used instead. An extra blanket can be useful either with or without the sleeping bag, once again depending on the climate you are in. And don't forget a comfy pillow.

# Cooking

Even though you may be a long way from home, there is no reason to miss out on yummy meals. If there is a stove in your gear, use it as you would at home.

Stoves with multiple burners as well as portable ovens are available along with cookbooks specifically for camp cooking, and a range of cookware.

Most stoves run on LPG (Liquid Petroleum Gas), often called propane, and connect to the stove via a flexible hose, while others run on butane. Propane is probably the most economical way to go, as the gas delivers more heat for the amount you use.

While both propane and butane are a type of LPG. The propane has to be stored at a much higher pressure than butane. Therefore, the bottles for propane are much heavier due to their construction

The bottles used to store propane come in several different sizes, generally from 1.25 kg up to 9 kg. The larger bottles can be quite heavy, so most people would choose a bottle around 2 kg or 3 kg. This would give about one to two weeks of use, depending on how often you cooked and for how long.

Butane stoves use a disposable cartridge which fits directly to the stove. They are much simpler to set up but are usually smaller in size, with only one burner, as that is all the cartridge will be able to run. Butane doesn't burn as hot as propane, especially in very cold weather. However, in most situations it will work quite well and is a more convenient stove to use.

You will also need a pot or pan and utensils, but keep them to a minimum. Unless there is a large group, try to take only one pot and one frypan. And only the utensils and plates for the number of people you are with. Porcelain plates and bowels will break. Enamel, stainless steel or melamine is much more practical. A few cooking utensils, a bucket and a washing bowl, a folding chair for each person and a small folding table will just about complete your camp set up.

## Campfire Cooking

It is not necessary to always have food cooked on a hot plate or frypan. Baking cakes and deserts, roasting meat and vegetables, soups and casseroles are all possible while camping.

Campfire cooking is a great way to prepare food, as it saves on gas and helps create a warm atmosphere around the camp. It may take a little practise to get used to the amount of heat needed to cook the food, and how the fire should be used to get the best results. Start with simple meals first, then as you get used to it, try something more complicated.

A common way to cook while camping is to use a camp oven. This is a cast iron pot which can be used on a stove or more often on a campfire. There are also ovens made from spun steel as well.

Personally, I prefer the steel ovens, as the lid can be turned over and used as a shallow frypan, while the base can act as a deep frypan or pot, and put together, you have your camp oven. They are also much lighter than cast iron, and because of the way the lid is designed it would be difficult to cook on the lid of a cast iron camp oven.

However, the cast iron oven is the more traditional one and is really good for keeping the heat in. The sides and bottom of the steel ovens are not as thick as the cast iron, and you have to be a bit more vigilant in making sure you don't burn your dinner, or lose the heat as well. I have used both with successes and failures. The trick is to monitor the heat of the fire.

It is important to use the right cookware, as flames and coals can create extreme heat that may damage some pot or pans. Camp ovens that are either cast iron or steel are the best. The same goes for frypans and pots. Always cook over coals rather than flames for best results.

Start your fire early so there is a good bed of hot coals available when you are ready to start cooking.

Once you have your coals, remove some to one side and sit your oven, pot or pan on these. Not too may coals to start with, remember they will be very hot. If you are using a camp oven, put the lid on and put some coals on top. This gives better heat inside the oven and cooks the food more evenly. Keep the campfire going so it would be able to replenish the coals as the others start to cool. There is no thermostat in campfires, so watch the cooking carefully to make sure all is under control.

It does take a little practise to get it right, so start with a little heat rather that a lot of heat, and monitor the cooking by occasionally removing the lid and checking your dinner. It is possible to cook almost anything in a camp oven. Roast meats, vegetables, bread and cakes. Try getting a camp oven cookbook to give you some helpful hints, then start cooking.

## Keeping Things Cool

One of the great debates in camping is whether to take an ice box or a portable fridge to keep food and drinks cool. An ice box is lot cheaper to buy than a fridge, even if you get a good quality one. If you are looking at an ice box, aim for quality. A good ice box will have much better insulation qualities than the cheaper ones and can keep ice up to 7 days in ideal conditions. Ideal conditions usually mean using solid ice on a day not more than around 30 degrees, keeping it out of the sun, starting with food that is already chilled and not keeping it in the back of a car that is parked in the sun.

Realistically though, you would expect to keep ice in a quality ice box for around 4 days on average, depending on how hot the weather is. In a less expensive ice box you would probably average 2 days.

The problem is getting ice in remote areas in Central and Northern Australia. This may mean you would have to enquire ahead as to the availability of ice. If proving to be difficult to get, then you may have to limit what type of fresh foods you will be carrying. A portable fridge, however, never needs ice and will continue to run happily on even the hottest days. What is needed is adequate battery power from your car.

Basically, there are three types of portable fridges on the Australian market. The most common is a compressor fridge which runs on either 12 volts, 24 volts or mains power, which is 240 volts. Most fridges use 12 volts, as it is the most common voltage cars use. However, larger vehicles, such as trucks, have 24 volt systems, so the fridge will adapt to the higher voltage automatically. Of course the 240 volt system is used in campsites when mains power is available.

The compressor fridge is the same system as a household fridge, being able to have the cabinet temperature adjusted from cool to freezing. Some units have a divider in the cabinet, meaning half can be fridge while the other half can be freezer.

Another type of fridge is the thermoelectric fridge. I would call this type an electric ice box. They will cool the food, but are limited to only around 20 degrees below ambient temperature. These units will not freeze, and would struggle on hot days. Best used for day trips or weekends, they are ideal to just keep things cool. An interesting feature of the thermoelectric fridge is that it can keep food warm as well. Some heating to around 60 degrees.

The third type of fridge is an absorption refrigerator, often referred to as a three-way fridge. This type of fridge has no moving parts when operating is completely silent. It will run on either propane, 12 volts or mains power. Basically, it operates by heating an ammonia and water mixture which turns to a vapour. It then goes through a process that absorbs heat from inside the cabinet, lowering the cabinet temperature.

It is commonly found in caravans and motor homes, and can be an upright fridge or a chest fridge. This design of fridge has been around for a long time, and used to be called a kerosene fridge because it used kerosene to heat the boiler with a small flame.

Unfortunately, this type of fridge can be a little fussy to operate, as in a very hot environment, they will not operate as well as a compressor fridge. They also need to be kept level, and well vented to allow the heat from the boiler to escape.

When operating on 12 volts, the fridge draws almost 6 amps, so it can drain a car battery reasonably quickly. For this reason, the 12 volt system is best utilised when the car is running, as in, travelling along. Then the car keeps the battery fully charged. Gas or mains power can then be used when stationary.

In a caravan or motor home the fridge is installed permanently, as it is designed to. But when camping with a tent, the fridge is generally a chest type and shouldn't be left inside the vehicle because of the heat it generates in operation. This is not a risk of causing a fire, but of filling the vehicle with fumes when operating on gas and creating an oven effect inside your car, which can affect the performance of the fridge.

# Water Solutions

In Australia, water is very precious. Not all camps have drinking water readily available. Bore water is more common, especially in the outback. Bore water is often heavily laden with dissolved minerals and can be a bit brackish and salty. It is not going to hurt you; it just won't taste very good. So it is often necessary to carry fresh drinking water in containers.

The general rule is to carry 5 litres of drinking water per person per day. This may differ depending on what region you are in, the time of year e.g. summer or winter, and how readily available fresh drinking water is.

For example, travelling through populated areas, good water could be collected from taps in camping grounds or picnic areas and often fuel stations, so you wouldn't have to carry as much. But in remote areas you would probably only get water from established caravan parks, which is connected to town water, as most picnic areas and other places would have bore water. If unsure, it would be advisable to ask someone before you fill any containers or taste it, you will soon notice the difference.

Most buildings in the outback towns would have a water tank to catch any rainwater and would be used for private use only. This water would rarely be available to the general public. As a backup, some people carry bottled water which they buy from supermarkets and use only for drinking.

## Washing and Toileting

When camping in an established campground, showers and flushing toilets are provided for your use, usually in a spacious and clean amenities block. One for the boys and one for the girls. But in a bush camp, there may only be pit toilets (commonly called "long drops"), and no showers, and in some cases there may be nothing at all.

If you are at one of these camps, then there are some things to be considered. Firstly, when going to the toilet, stay at least 50 meters from any water course to prevent anything from being washed into the water. Any solid waste should be buried at least 20 to 30 cm deep, so take a small shovel with you. Dig yourself a hole, then squat over it, making sure all the used toilet paper goes in the hole as well, then fill it in. Sometimes the ground can be hard and rocky. Persevere, because if it isn't deep enough, animals will dig it up leaving a mess that attracts flies and is unsightly. In some cases people burn the paper, but be very careful, as a breeze can blow burning paper into dry bush and you may have a bush fire on your hands.

Urine doesn't need to be buried, but don't leave any toilet paper to be blown around by the wind. It is not very pleasant to have used toilet paper blowing through your camp, especially when you're having lunch. Wrap the wet toilet paper in some extra paper and take it back to your camp to be put in the rubbish.

Of course, hygiene is very important in the bush, getting a tummy bug when you are a long way from medical help is not what you want, so it is important to wash your hands or use a sanitising gel whenever you go to the toilet.

This is often the reason why people don't go camping. Some find the whole thing inconvenient and embarrassing, especially if you have to go looking for a suitable bush to squat behind. There is also the fear of being accidently discovered by someone, when you are exposed in a very personal situation. Washing can also be difficult for some, for the same reasons as toileting, as well as having to heat water then stand naked somewhere in order to wash.

One easy way round all this is to take an en suite tent. These tents are usually of a pop-up type that is erected in minutes. Into this, you can put a small flushing chemical toilet so you can have privacy as well as convenience. They can also be used as a shower tent.

There are a variety of portable showers available these days, some have a small submersible pump that is placed in a bucket of warm water and others have a gas heater that heats the water as you go. Of course the simplest way is a bucket of warm water and wash cloth to sponge yourself down. It certainly makes you feel much better.

## Power Solutions

Today's modern technology means it is possible to take all sorts of electronic gadgets with us on camping trips. But keeping these devices powered up can be a bit of an issue. The electrical devices I am talking about are things like TVs, computers, fridges, and lights, which do not have disposable batteries.

Some visitors from overseas will have personal equipment that runs on a different voltage, and may have a different shaped plug. So it would be necessary to include an appropriate adaptor to suit. Almost all of the electric equipment used in camping will need either one of these two power sources to either run the unit or recharge the batteries. In a campground where power is available, it should be easy to keep the batteries charged; however, when bush camping, then a different method will be required.

At this point, I want to explain the difference between volts, amps and watts, as all electrical devices will have these on an identification label somewhere on the device. Voltage is the pressure that causes the current to flow along the wire. We measure the rate of flow of electricity as an electric current and measure it in Amperes, and a Watt is a measure of how much energy is released per second from the current. Understanding the difference will help to decide what size battery will run what device and for how long. It can also help to work out the best way to recharge the battery to prevent it from going flat.

Recharging or running any electric device off your vehicle's battery is most common. However, how long the battery will run the device depends on its capacity. If you are not careful, continuous use of your vehicle's batteries may result in a flat battery and not being able to start your car, which can be a little annoying when you are a long way from help.

One way to overcome this is to periodically start your vehicle and allow it to idle for a while until the battery is recharged. This works well if you are moving each day, but if you are staying put for several days at a time it would become a bit of a nuisance.

Adding a second battery to your vehicle overcomes this, as the auxiliary battery can go completely flat without affecting your starting battery. Usually the system is set up so that as soon as you start the engine, the auxiliary battery will be recharged. But you would still be limited to the capacity of the auxiliary battery, and the vehicle would still need to be started to recharge this battery. How long your vehicle's battery lasts will depend on what capacity it is and how much current is being drawn out of it.

Another charging method would be with a generator. These units can not only recharge batteries, but run your devices as well. They can be very small and easy to carry and use. Also modern generators are much quieter than their earlier cousins.

However, generators still give off some noise as well as exhaust fumes, and some owners leave them running for long periods of time, even overnight. This can be very annoying to other campers who want some peace and quiet and fresh air. The result of this is that all national parks and state forests and a whole lot of other campgrounds have banned generators outright. They can be expensive to buy and you will need to carry extra fuel for them as well.

Solar panels are probably the most common way to recharge batteries. There are different types and sizes to suit different charging options. They are much cheaper to buy these days and cost nothing to run. Getting the right size will, of course, depend on your individual needs. This can be a little complicated, so it needs to be calculated by someone in the know, who can explain the best size panel to use. Once you have this sorted, they are an easy to use and efficient way to charge batteries.

Obviously they need the sun to operate properly, so a cloudy day will mean that they will not put out their maximum amperage. Also, the angle of the sun will affect the amount of output the panel will have. A solar panel can continually charge a battery to the point of overcharging and "cooking" the battery causing permanent damage. Therefore, all panels need a voltage regulator. That way, when the panel has fully charged the battery, the regulator will cut the amount of current from the panel and preserve the battery.

A solar panel is a charging device, it will not be able to properly run any device, because the current output will vary according to how it sits with the sun. But hook it up to a suitable battery and the panel can replace what the battery loses when supplying power for your electrical needs.

## Getting Underway

So you have worked out how you are travelling and what type of tent/caravan/camper/motor home/whatever, you are taking. Your vehicle is in good nick and you have everything you need. Now you have to pack your gear in the vehicle. Try to imagine arriving at your campsite and getting your camp set up. Ask yourself, what do I need first? The first thing you want should be easiest to get at without having to dig around looking for it. If tenting, this would be the ground sheet and tent or swag, followed by bedding. In the case of a caravan or camper trailer, the trailer may need to be uncoupled first, and attached to any services, followed by table and chairs. It may be time then for a hot cuppa or cold beer or wine and some dinner. So cooking gear will have to be set up.

If you have followed the rule of keeping things simple, all of this should take less than half an hour. Some of your gear may not be needed every time, so it can stay packed in the car, out of the way, for access later. When repacking, do it all in reverse, that way the next time you set up camp, it will all be in order of what is needed first.

I have already talked about fridges and ice boxes, but other foods also need to be stored. In a caravan or similar, there are cupboards or storage bins often built in. In a station wagon, some people have drawer systems fitted in the rear. Plastic tubs can also be used. These are relatively inexpensive and come in lots of different sizes. They can also be used for general storage as they keep everything tidy and in place.

# Chapter Five
## Where to Stay

Road trips in Australia are very popular. Consequently, there are many choices when it comes to finding somewhere to stop for the night. Almost every town has a caravan park or campground, or motel or pub if that is your choice. Obviously, some will be better than others and you may have to decide if it is worth staying or moving on.

Caravan parks offer the best options, especially for families with young children. Showers, toilets, playgrounds, barbeques, camp kitchens are generally the normal thing and you are usually close to town facilities as well. They can get very busy though especially around school holidays, which may mean lining up for the showers or barbeques.

Camping in National parks or reserves is quite popular, with some very scenic campgrounds and good facilities. Some campgrounds are in remote country and only offer a cleared area to camp in, with pit toilets as the only facility.

While these campgrounds are basic, they do offer activities, such as bushwalking or photographing wildlife that often comes right up to your camp. Of course there will be fees for these places, which will vary due to location and facilities on offer.

Often it is possible to stay at roadside stops. If you are considering this and you want to get some sleep, try to get as far back from the road as possible, as trucks often travel all night and they can be noisy as they pass by. Some of these stops are specifically for trucks. It would be a good idea to avoid these ones because the trucks may arrive or leave anytime through the night.

In the outback it is sometimes possible to bush camp. This is not in any campground or park but often off the side of the road, in the bush, and with no facilities at all. In this case, look for a spot several hundred meters off the road. If you are on your own, you may not feel comfortable doing this. But if you are with others, you will feel much more secure, and enjoy the tranquillity. I have camped by myself many times and never felt threatened. Often other travellers may see your camp, and camp nearby as they are also looking for a safe campsite.

Sometimes bush camping will be on crown land, which have no restrictions, other times it may be on private property. Here permission should be sought from the property owners or managers. The problem with the outback is that the homestead may be many kilometres away and you won't know where it is. In this case show some respect to the property owner and don't damage any fences or farm property, don't cut down trees for firewood (some people do this) or camp near waterholes, tanks or bores, as livestock may need to get to it to drink. If you want a camp fire, use only fallen timber and keep the fire small. Practise good toileting techniques as I explained earlier, and take all rubbish with you when you leave.

# Looking After Yourself

On a long road trip, it is easy to not think about basic health and wellbeing. General health issues can crop up because we are in holiday mode and are only thinking of enjoying ourselves.

Being outside for most of the day means we are exposed to the elements, much more than at home. The Australian sun can be harsh, drying our skin, hair, and causing sunburn. A dry wind can have similar effects.

When it is sunny and warm, there is nothing wrong in getting a bit of sun. In fact, our bodies need sunlight to keep us healthy. However, it is easy to get too much sun, and burn.

For prolonged exposure to sun and wind, it is important to cover up under a wide brimmed hat, and if you don't want to wear long sleeve shirts or long trousers because it is hot, then use an appropriate sun block on any exposed areas of the skin.

A good diet is also necessary. Fresh foods are readily available and with modern portable refrigeration, fruit and vegetables can be easily carried, as can fresh meat. It would be a whole lot cheaper too. So don't get into the habit of buying junk food because it is easier than preparing a proper meal. Eating the wrong foods all the time means you won't have the proper nutrition, which can result in you not feeling the best, especially when you are being active. And drink plenty of water.

I have already mentioned practising good hygiene when toileting. But also when preparing and cooking food. This is not about accidently getting a bit of dirt in your dinner, it is about keeping utensils clean and cooking your food properly. A common source of food poisoning is poorly prepared or under cooked food.

Be aware of where you are and what you are doing. Australia is a big place with many, very remote areas. Even in an emergency, help could be hours away. So don't take unnecessary risks, like climbing a cliff to get a better picture, or blindly walking through long grass, when there may be snakes present.

Fast flowing rivers are also a hazard, as they may be deeper than you think. So if something bad does happen, stay calm. Try to think logically about how to deal with the situation at hand. Doing a first aid course before you leave on your trip is a good idea, and carry a decent first aid kit. That way you may be able to relieve some of the suffering of an injury, or even preserve a life while waiting for help to arrive.

## Finally

Some people spend several years travelling in caravans or campers around the continent. Mostly they are older and either retired or on long service leave, also, families may take time off work, and travel with their children, showing them so many different places and people, and having different experiences they would not normally have at home.

With so many worries we seem to have today, it is nice to know that it is still possible to steal away from reality every now and then. To leave behind the phones and meetings and day-to-day pressures that modern life brings. Of course, these pressures have been with us for many years. Even our parents and grandparents had things to worry them, perhaps in a different way to today, but they were still there.

In Australia, Caravanning and camping are very popular. Having just a weekend trip or perhaps a couple of weeks away at a time, is to a lot of people the best way to relax and have a holiday. A way to escape those pressures. Whether you are touring the outback or spending a week camped at the beach, either in a holiday park or in a bush setting, you will always find people out there enjoying the great outdoors.